Humpback Whale

GIANTS of the OCEAN

Jack Zayarny

MEDIA ENHANCED BOOKS
AV²
BY WEIGL
ADDED VALUE · AUDIO VISUAL
www.av2books.com

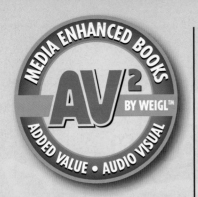

AV² provides enriched content that supplements and complements this book. Weigl's AV² books strive to create inspired learning and engage young minds in a total learning experience.

Your AV² Media Enhanced books come alive with...

Audio
Listen to sections of the book read aloud.

Key Words
Study vocabulary, and complete a matching word activity.

Go to **www.av2books.com**, and enter this book's unique code.

Video
Watch informative video clips.

Quizzes
Test your knowledge.

BOOK CODE

D976449

Embedded Weblinks
Gain additional information for research.

Slide Show
View images and captions, and prepare a presentation.

AV² by Weigl brings you media enhanced books that support active learning.

Try This!
Complete activities and hands-on experiments.

... and much, much more!

Published by AV2 by Weigl.
350 5th Avenue, 59th Floor New York, NY 10118
Website: www.av2books.com www.weigl.com

Library of Congress Cataloging-in-Publication Data

Zayarny, Jack, author.
 Humpback whales / Jack Zayarny.
    pages cm. -- (Giants of the ocean)
 ISBN 978-1-4896-1078-2 (hardcover : alk. paper) -- ISBN 978-1-4896-1079-9 (softcover : alk. paper) -- ISBN 978-1-4896-1080-5 (single user ebk.) -- ISBN 978-1-4896-1081-2 (multi user ebk.)
 1. Humpback whale--Juvenile literature. 2. Whales--Juvenile literature. I. Title.
 QL737.C424Z39 2015
 599.5'25--dc23

                            2014004526

Printed in the United States of America in North Mankato, Minnesota
1 2 3 4 5 6 7 8 9 0 18 17 16 15 14

042014
WEP150314

Weigl acknowledges Getty Images as the primary image supplier for this title.

Project Coordinator: Heather Kissock
Designer: Mandy Christiansen

Contents

Meet the Humpback Whale

Humpback whales are large ocean **mammals**. The humpback whale gets its name from the shape its body makes as it dives into the water. Humpbacks are best known for their "songs" that they use to communicate with each other.

Like all mammals, humpback whales breathe air with lungs. This means that they need to reach the ocean's surface to breathe. A humpback whale uses two holes in its back for this. These holes are called blowholes.

The humpback whale is black or gray on the upper side of its body and white on its underside. It has a large head covered with bumps called tubercles. Scientists believe tubercles can help whales swim better.

Humpback whales have flippers that can be as long as one-third the length of their bodies. The whales are known for acrobatic tricks, such as breaching. Breaching is when a whale jumps out of the water. Some scientists believe that the whales do this to stun their prey or to remove **parasites** from the skin.

Adult humpback whales can remain underwater for as long as 45 minutes at a time.

All About Humpback Whales

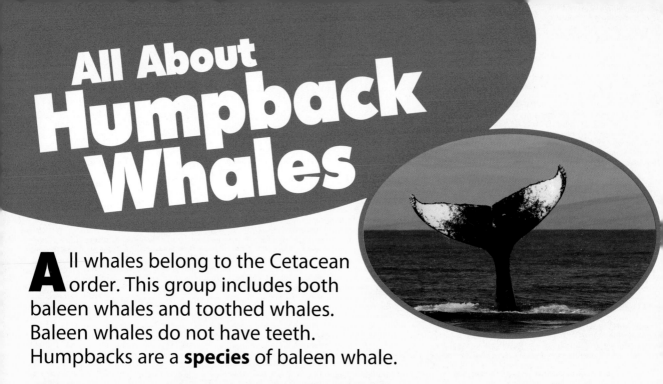

All whales belong to the Cetacean order. This group includes both baleen whales and toothed whales. Baleen whales do not have teeth. Humpbacks are a **species** of baleen whale.

Where Humpback Whales Live

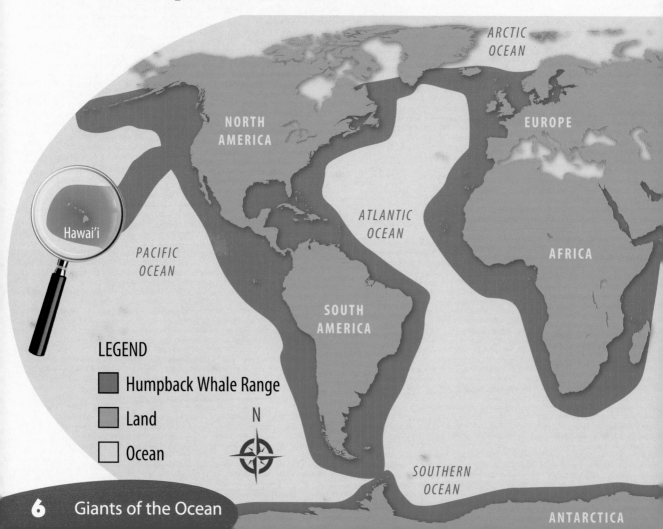

ARCTIC OCEAN

NORTH AMERICA

EUROPE

Hawai'i

ATLANTIC OCEAN

PACIFIC OCEAN

AFRICA

SOUTH AMERICA

LEGEND

☐ Humpback Whale Range

☐ Land

☐ Ocean

N

SOUTHERN OCEAN

ANTARCTICA

Instead of teeth, baleen whales have many hard bristles called baleen in their mouths. These bristles catch and filter food. Baleen whales feed on large amounts of small ocean animals, such as **krill** and fish.

Although they share many of the same traits as other baleen whales, humpback whales are unique. Humpbacks are the only species in their **genus**, Megaptera. The name Megaptera means "big wings" and refers to the humpback's large fins.

48 feet long
(14 meters)

Can weigh
up to

40
Tons
(36 tonnes)

Humpback whales shut off half of their brain to sleep. The other half controls their breathing.

ORCAS **are the humpback's only natural predator.**

Classifying Humpback Whales

ORDER
Cetaceans

FAMILY
Baleen Whales

GENUS
Megaptera

SPECIES
Novaeangliae

(Humpback Whales)

ASIA

PACIFIC
OCEAN

INDIAN
OCEAN

ASIA

The Home of Humpback Whales

Humpback whales live in oceans all around the world. They can be found as far north as Greenland and as far south as Antarctica. Humpback whales spend most of their time in coastal waters. They also like areas where there are underwater mountains and ridges. These areas are called shelf waters.

The **longest** recorded **distance** of a humpback whale's migration is **6,200 miles** (10,000 kilometers).

Humpback whales prefer warm temperatures. In the summer, they prefer to stay in northern areas where the water is cooler. In the winter, humpbacks **migrate** to more tropical waters in the south. When the humpback whale migrates, it travels through deep water.

Humpback whales travel the same route every year. Humpbacks that spend their winters off the coast of Hawai'i and their summers in Alaska. They then return to the Hawai'ian islands the following winter. This round-trip is one of the longest migrations of any animal species.

Humpback whales can dive underwater as deep as 500 feet (152 m).

Features of Humpback Whales

Humpback whales have developed many **adaptations** that help them to survive. They move very well for such large creatures and are well suited to live in a variety of ocean environments.

BALEEN
Baleen is used to trap krill and other small creatures in the whale's mouth while letting the water out. Baleen bristles are made of keratin, the same material as human fingernails and hair.

FLIPPERS
Humpback whales have the largest flippers of any whale species. The flippers help the whale travel, catch its food, and jump out of the water.

BODY
Humpback whales have long, rounded bodies. Their skin is smooth and rubbery. Underneath the skin is a thick layer of fat called blubber. Blubber helps keep the whale warm in cold waters.

TAIL
Humpback whales are powerful swimmers. Their large tail fins are called flukes. Whales use their flukes to push out of the water when breaching.

Diet of Humpback Whales

Humpback whales are **omnivores**. They feed mostly on krill, **plankton**, and small fish. Humpbacks are filter feeders. To eat, a humpback swims into a school of prey animals with an open mouth, catching as many as possible. Then, the whale closes its mouth and filters the water out through its two rows of baleen plates. The fish, krill, or plankton remain trapped inside.

Humpback whales have a unique way of hunting called bubble net feeding. To form a bubble net, many whales swim in a large circle beneath an area where there are many plankton or krill. They blow a wall of bubbles as they swim in a spiral path. This wall of bubbles floats up, trapping the whales' prey inside the bubble net. The whales can then easily feed on large amounts of prey at once.

Humpbacks are seasonal feeders. They eat large amounts of food in the summer to build up blubber, and eat very little in winter. The blubber provides energy to the whale and helps it survive the winter.

A humpback whale's **blubber** layer can be up to **6 inches** (15 cm) **thick**.

An adult humpback whale can eat 4,400 to 5,500 pounds (2,000 to 2,500 kilograms) of krill, plankton, and fish every day.

Life Cycle of Humpback Whales

Humpback whales mate in the winter. The mother gives birth to a calf within 11 to 12 months. The newborn humpback whale can be up to 16 feet (4.9 m) long. The baby humpback weighs 2.5 tons (2.8 t) at birth.

Humpback whale young are called calves. Mothers are called cows. Mother and calf humpback whales have the strongest bond in humpback society. They will stay together for up to a year while the calf grows. Male humpback whales do not help raise calves. Another humpback, called an escort, will live with the mother and calf. This escort can be a female, but is usually a male. A group of humpback whales that live together is called a pod.

A mother humpback produces about 100 pounds (45 kg) of milk each day to feed her calf.

The Cycle

Whales Mate
Humpback whales can mate when they are about 7 years old.

Calf Becomes Adult
Adult humpbacks can live 45 to 50 years.

Female Whale Becomes Pregnant
Female humpbacks can have calves every two to four years.

Calf Develops
The calf swims with its mother and drinks her milk for one year. After this, it travels with other whales of the same age.

Humpback Calf Is Born
The calf floats to the surface to take its first breath. Within 30 minutes, it learns how to swim.

History of Humpback Whales

Whales have been on the Earth for millions of years. All whales come from a common ancestor who lived on Earth more than 38 million years ago. The first baleen whales did not appear on Earth until 25 million years ago.

In 1781, Georg Borowski gave the humpback whale its scientific name. It was assigned the name *megaptera novaeangliae*. This means "big-winged New Englander." Humpback whales were given this name because of their large flippers and because they were often seen off the coast of New England.

The humpback whale came very close to extinction. In the 20th century, more than 95 percent of the humpback population was killed. The whales were killed for their blubber, baleen, or simply for sport. To save the species, humpback whaling was banned worldwide by the **International Whaling Commission** in 1966. Today, the ban continues, and humpback whale numbers are increasing again.

More than **200,000** humpback whales were hunted and killed in the 19th and 20th centuries.

Humpback whales were often hunted for their oil. Whale oil can be used as a source of fuel.

Encounters with Humpback Whales

People all over the world enjoy seeing the acrobatic antics of the humpback whale. Organizations, such as the Pacific Whale Foundation, offer tours that take people out on the ocean to observe the whales in their natural **habitat**. These tours teach people safe ways to interact with the humpback whale. The money earned from the tours provides funding for research.

Humpback **whale songs** can be **heard** from **up to 50 miles** (80 km) **away**.

One of the most important areas of research involves the humpback whale's songs. In 1971, Roger Payne and Scott McVay were the first scientists to describe the humpback whale song. Known for their recognizable pattern, the songs are made up of five to seven themes that are repeated in order. Some scientists believe humpback whales sing to attract mates. Others think that these songs are meant to mark a male humpback's territory. Studies continue to determine the reason for the sounds.

Another area of scientific research involves studying the whale's fluke. Each humpback whale has unique features on its fluke. These features allow scientists to identify each whale and study its behavior. This has helped scientists monitor humpback whale populations and migration patterns.

Humpback whales are curious creatures. They will often approach unfamiliar objects in their territory, including scientists.

Conservation

The **International Union for Conservation of Nature (IUCN)** has listed the humpback whale as endangered on its Red List of Threatened Species. However, in recent years, governments and organizations have worked together to help the humpback whale. These efforts have led to a rise in the whale population in many areas. In 1996, for example, there were as few as 1,400 humpback whales living the North Pacific. Today, there are about 20,000 humpback whales in that region.

There are several laws that help protect humpbacks. The 1973 Endangered Species Act in the U.S. was designed to help protect the humpback and other endangered animals from hunters. This law prevents people from hunting the whales in American waters.

Myths and Legends

The Story of Paikea and Ruatapu

Paikea was the favorite son of Chief Uenuku.
This made Paikea's older brother Ruatapu jealous. Ruatapu decided to kill Paikea and to tell his father that Paikea had drowned while fishing in their canoe.

Ruatapu made a hole in the bottom of the canoe and filled the hole with chips of wood. In the morning, Paikea, Ruatapu, and their brothers went fishing in the canoe. When they were a long way out to sea, Ruatapu pushed aside the chips of wood from the hole. Water rushed in, flooding the canoe. All the brothers fell into the sea and drowned, except Paikea and Ruatapu.

Ruatapu swam after Paikea to grab him, but Paikea was too fast. "I will not drown" Paikea said. "I am descended from Tangaroa, the god of the sea, and he will help me." Tangaroa heard Paikea and sent a humpback whale named Tohora to take him to land. Paikea escaped from Ruatapu on the back of the whale.

In a rage, Ruatapu used a magic spell that sent five giant waves rolling across the ocean after Paikea. Tohora was too fast, and the waves could not catch him. The waves hit the shore and then went back to Ruatapu. Ruatapu drowned. Paikea was safe.

Test Your Knowledge

There are many different whale species in the world's oceans. The activity below will help you learn more about the different types of these mammals. You will need two blank sheets of paper and a pencil or pen.

Materials

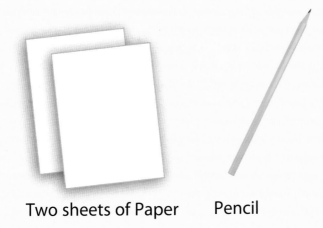

Two sheets of Paper   Pencil

1 Using this book and other resources, read about different species of whales and their characteristics.

2 Now, using what you have learned, draw a picture of four different whale species on the first sheet of paper. Label your drawings with the name of each type of whale.

3 On the second sheet of paper, write down the species of the whales you drew across the top. Then, in point form, write down how these species are similar and different from one another.

Quiz

1 What are the bumps on a humpback's head called?

2 Which other whale is the humpback's only natural predator?

3 What is it called when humpback whales jump out of the water?

4 What order do humpback whales belong to?

5 How do scientists usually identify individual humpback whales?

6 What are young humpback whales called?

7 Why were humpback whales hunted by humans?

8 How many themes is a humpback whale song usually made of?

9 In what year did the humpback whale receive its scientific name?

10 How long does the humpback whale calf stay with its mother?

Answers:
1. Tubercles 2. The orca
3. Breaching 4. Cetaceans
5. By their flukes 6. Calves
7. Blubber, sport, and baleen
8. Five to seven 9. 1781
10. Up to a year

Key Words

adaptations: changes that help an animal or plant survive

genus: a subdivision of an animal family

habitat: the natural environment of an organism

International Union for Conservation of Nature (IUCN): the largest and oldest organization in the world dedicated to conserving the environment

International Whaling Commission: an organization the goal of which is to protect whale populations

krill: a small shrimp-like animal

mammals: a group of animals that breathe air with lungs and give birth to live babies

migrate: to move from one place to another

omnivores: animals that eat both plants and other animals

parasites: organisms that live on or inside other organisms

plankton: very small plants and animals that float in oceans and lakes

species: a group of animals or plants that share similar features

Index

Log on to www.av2books.com

AV² by Weigl brings you media enhanced books that support active learning. Go to www.av2books.com, and enter the special code found on page 2 of this book. You will gain access to enriched and enhanced content that supplements and complements this book. Content includes video, audio, weblinks, quizzes, a slide show, and activities.

AV² Online Navigation

Audio
Listen to sections of the book read aloud.

Book Pages
AV² pages directly correspond to pages in the book.

Video
Watch informative video clips.

Key Words
Study vocabulary, and complete a matching word activity.

Embedded Weblinks
Gain additional information for research.

Quizzes
Test your knowledge.

Slide Show
View images and captions, and prepare a presentation.

Try This!
Complete activities and hands-on experiments.

AV² was built to bridge the gap between print and digital. We encourage you to tell us what you like and what you want to see in the future.

Sign up to be an AV² Ambassador at www.av2books.com/ambassador.